롤러코스터
이래서 강력추천합니다!

체계적인 학습 | 초등학교 교육 과정을 충실히 반영하고 교과서 지문을 최대한 활용함으로써 학생들이 배워야 할 주요 학습 내용을 체계적으로 익힐 수 있도록 하였습니다.

학년별 맞춤 학습 | 모든 학년에서 표현과 낱말 학습을 기본으로 하되, 1·2학년은 Phonics, 3·4학년은 Reading & Writing, 5·6학년은 Grammar를 다루는 등, 각 학년별 주요 학습 영역을 중점적으로 다룸으로써 학년별 맞춤 학습을 추구하였습니다.

균형적인 학습 | 읽기, 쓰기 학습뿐만 아니라 오디오 CD와 동영상 CD를 활용한 듣기, 말하기 학습을 통해 영어의 4개 영역(Listening, Speaking, Reading, Writing)을 고루 마스터할 수 있도록 하였습니다.

자발적인 학습 | Song, Chant를 통해 표현을 자연스럽게 익히고, Cartoon을 통해 배운 내용을 재미있게 정리하는 등 다양한 Activity를 통해 학생들이 흥미를 가지고 적극적으로 수업에 참여할 수 있도록 하였습니다.

동영상을 통한 원어민과의 학습 | 원어민의 발음과 입모양을 동영상 CD를 통해 정확히 인지하고 학습자의 발음을 녹음해 원어민의 발음과 비교하여 들어 보게 함으로써 학습자 스스로 발음을 교정할 수 있는 기회를 제공하였습니다.

01 Student Book_ Unit 1, 3

Conversation

초등영어 교과과정과 연계된 표현을 학습하고,
다양한 활동을 통해 표현을 익혀 봐요.

Words

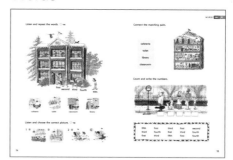

생활 영어 표현과 관련된 낱말을 학습하고,
재미있게 낱말을 익혀 봐요.

Reading

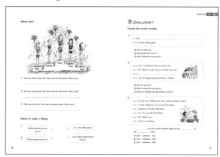

표현에 대한 이해력을 높이고, 각종 경시대회 및
TOEFL iBT에 대비할 수 있는 문제를 풀어 봐요.

Writing

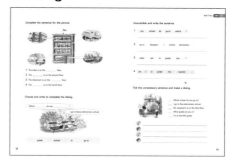

학습한 표현을 써 보면서, 자유롭게 활용할 수
있는 능력을 키워 봐요.

Cartoon

재미있는 만화를 통해 이미 학습한 표현과
낱말을 종합 정리해 봐요.

Test

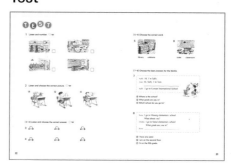

테스트를 통해 학습한 표현 및 낱말에 대한
학습 성취도를 점검해 봐요.

Student Book_ Unit 2, 4

Cartoon

재미있는 만화를 통해 앞으로 배울 핵심 문법
사항을 미리 알아봐요.

Grammar point 1

핵심 문법 사항을 익히고 다양한 활동을 통해
응용해 봐요.

Grammar point 2

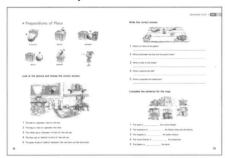

핵심 문법 사항을 익히고 다양한 활동을 통해
응용해 봐요.

Story

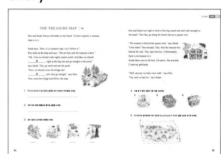

학습한 문법을 활용한 흥미로운 이야기를 읽고
문제를 풀어 봐요.

Story words

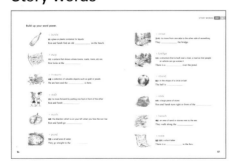

이야기에서 학습한 낱말을 예문을 통해
종합 정리해 봐요.

Test

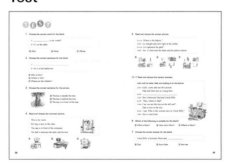

테스트를 통해 학습한 문법에 대한 이해도와
응용력을 평가해 봐요.

02 Workbook

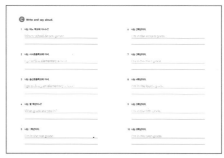

낱말을 따라 쓴 다음, 우리말에 해당하는
낱말을 직접 써 봐요.

표현을 따라 쓴 다음, 우리말에 해당하는
표현을 직접 써 봐요.

잘 듣고, 빈칸에 알맞은 낱말과
표현을 자신있게 써 봐요.

03 권말 테스트

낱말 및 표현에 관한 문제를 풀면서 그동안 쌓은
실력을 마음껏 발휘해 봐요.
(Achievement Test / Final Test)

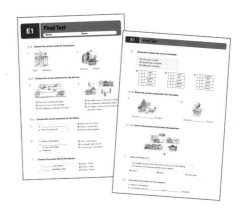

04 동영상 CD

Conversation

초등영어 교과과정과 연계된 표현을 배워 봐요.

Words

생활영어 표현과 관련된 낱말을 배워 봐요.

Speak

학습한 낱말들을 녹음해 원어민의 발음과
비교해 봐요.

05 오디오 CD

Student Book, Workbook의 내용과 노래 및
챈트가 담겨 있어요.

Learning Points

E1

Unit Title	Theme	Function (Unit 1&3) Grammar (Unit 2&4)	Conversation (Unit 1&3) Language Item (Unit 2&4)
❶ I'm in the Fifth Grade	School	· Talking about which school someone goes to · Asking about one's grade	Which school do you go to? I go to Sisa elementary school. What grade are you in? I'm in the fifth grade.
❷ What Floor Are You on?	What & Number	· Question word: what · Understanding cardinal and ordinal numbers	What does your brother do? What time is it now? first, second, third, fourth, fifth, …
❸ Where's the Bookstore?	Places	· Asking about directions	Where's the bookstore? Go straight and turn left at the corner. It's next to the library.
❹ Where Are My Glasses?	Where & Preposition	· Question word: where · Understanding the meaning of various prepositions	Where is Kevin? in front of, behind, between, next to, opposite

E2

Unit Title	Theme	Function(Unit 1&3) Grammar(Unit 2&4)	Conversation(Unit 1&3) Language Item(Unit 2&4)
1 What Seasons Do You Like?	Seasons	· Talking about favorite seasons · Talking about the activities in each season	What seasons do you like? I like fall and winter. What do you do in the winter? I go sledding.
2 Is Jane a Good Girl and Is Nick a Good Boy?	Conjunction & Negative	· Conjunction: and & but · Negative: don't & doesn't	I like cherries, and Katie likes cherries. I like apples, but John doesn't like apples. I have a book, but (I) don't read it.
3 My Birthday Is on Children's Day	Birthday	· Talking about birthday · Talking about what one wants for a birthday present	When is your birthday? My birthday is on Children's Day. What do you want for a present? I want a game CD.
4 When Is Your Birthday?	When & Preposition	· Question word: when · Prepositions of time: on & at	When is your birthday? My birthday is on Children's Day.

E3

Unit Title	Theme	Function(Unit 1&3) Grammar(Unit 2&4)	Conversation(Unit 1&3) Language Item(Unit 2&4)
1 May I Open the Window?	Can & May	· Permission using 'can' and 'may'	May I open the window? No, you may not.
2 You May Not Do That	Can & May	· Modal verb 'can' · Modal verb 'may'	Kevin can play the violin. You can use my computer. You may open the window.
3 Do You Have Any Bread?	Some & Any	· Expressing possession with 'some' and 'any'	Do you have any bread? No, I don't have any bread. I have some cookies.
4 How Sweet You Are!	Adjectives & Admiring	· Understanding the meaning of various adjectives · Admiring with 'how' and 'what'	I am busy. I have a long muffler. How kind (you are)! What a nice restaurant (it is)!

E4

Unit Title	Theme	Function (Unit 1&3) Grammar (Unit 2&4)	Conversation (Unit 1&3) Language Item (Unit 2&4)
❶ What Does Your Mom Do?	Occupation	· Talking about occupations	What does your mom do? My mom is a police officer. She catches thieves.
❷ Anything Wrong?	'Do' verb	· Positive, negative and question sentences with 'do' verb	He likes apples. She doesn't like ice cream. Does he want new shoes?
❸ How Was Your Weekend?	Past tense of 'be' verb	· Expressing the past tense	How was your weekend? It was terrible. I was sick in bed.
❹ Were You at Home Yesterday?	Past tense of 'be' verb	· Past tense of 'be' verb	I was sick yesterday. He wasn't absent from school. Was she an excellent pilot? Where were you yesterday?

E5

Unit Title	Theme	Function (Unit 1&3) Grammar (Unit 2&4)	Conversation (Unit 1&3) Language Item (Unit 2&4)
❶ I Cooked Lunch with Dad	Past tense of regular verbs	· Expressing the past tense	I cooked lunch with Dad, washed the dishes and cleaned the room.
❷ Did You Bring Harry Along?	Past tense of regular verbs	· Past tense of regular verbs	I cleaned the house yesterday. I did not (didn't) play baseball. Did you play the violin?
❸ What Did You Do Yesterday?	Past tense of irregular verbs	· Expressing the past tense	What did you do yesterday? I went to the concert.
❹ Did He Have a Perfect Day?	Past tense of irregular verbs	· Past tense of irregular verbs	We saw the stars last night. Where did you go on your vacation? I went to Jeju island.

E6

Unit Title	Theme	Function (Unit 1&3) / Grammar (Unit 2&4)	Conversation (Unit 1&3) / Language Item (Unit 2&4)
① I Must Go to the Dentist	Must	· Expressing one's duty	I must go to the dentist. I must take medicine.
② You Must Come Back Home by 12	Must & Have to	· Modal verbs 'must', 'have to'	I must do my homework. You must not eat too many sweets. Must I clean the room now? I have to go home now.
③ I Will Visit Uncle Tom's Farm	Future tense with 'will'	· Talking about the future	I will visit Uncle Tom's farm. I will take a trip to Hawaii with my family.
④ What Will You Do This Weekend?	Future tense with 'will'	· Modal verb 'will'	Tomorrow I will buy a scarf for Mom's birthday. I will not eat out this evening. Will you come here by 5? What will Silvia do this Sunday?

Roller Coaster

Contents

UNIT **1** **What Seasons Do You Like?** · 12

Conversation | Words
Reading | Writing
Cartoon | Test

UNIT **2** **Is Jane a Good Girl
and Is Nick a Good Boy?** · 24

Cartoon | Grammar Point 1
Grammar Point 2 | Story
Story Words | Test

UNIT **3** **My Birthday Is on Children's Day** · 36

Conversation | Words
Reading | Writing
Cartoon | Test

UNIT **4** **When Is Your Birthday?** · 48

Cartoon | Grammar Point 1
Grammar Point 2 | Story
Story Words | Test

Listening Script & Answers · 61

Appendix

1 Workbook
2 Achievement Test / Final Test

What Seasons Do You Like?

Listen and repeat the dialog. T02

 What seasons do you like?

 I like fall and winter.

 I like winter, too. I make snowmen and enjoy snow fights in the winter.
What do you do in the winter?

 I go sledding.

Speak aloud. T03

1

spring and summer / summer

swim in the swimming pool

2

spring and fall / spring

go on a picnic

Listen and choose the correct picture. T04

1 ⓐ    ⓑ    ⓒ

2 ⓐ    ⓑ    ⓒ

Listen and choose the correct answer. T05

1 *A:* _____

   B: I like summer and winter.

2 *A:* What do you do in the spring?

   B: _____

Listen and choose the correct dialog. T06

Listen and repeat the words. T07

spring

summer

swim
in the swimming pool

go on a picnic

fall

winter

go ice skating

read a book

go sledding

Listen and choose the correct picture. T08

1 ⓐ   ⓑ   2 ⓐ   ⓑ

Write the correct answer for the picture.

1  ☐

2  ☐

3  ☐

ⓐ go ice skating   ⓑ go sledding   ⓒ read a book

ⓓ go on a picnic   ⓔ swim in the swimming pool

Look at the picture and fill in the blanks.

1 I r____d books in the s____ing.

2 I s____m in the swimming ___oo__ in the s__m_____.

3 I go ___ a __ic__ic in the f____l.

4 I ____ ice ____ating in the ___ __nt____.

Choose the correct sentence.

1

    ⓐ She goes sledding.
    ⓑ She goes to school.
    ⓒ She goes ice skating.

2

    ⓐ He writes a letter.
    ⓑ He reads a book.
    ⓒ He sleeps in the bed.

3

    ⓐ They eat lunch.
    ⓑ They go to the zoo.
    ⓒ They go on a picnic.

4

    ⓐ She swims at the beach.
    ⓑ She swims in the swimming pool.
    ⓒ She drinks water in the swimming pool.

Match to make a dialog.

1 What seasons do you like?   I go on a picnic.

2 What do you do in the spring?   I like spring and summer.

⊙ CHALLENGE!

Choose the correct answer.

1

> *A:* What season do you like?
>
> *B:* _____

   ⓐ I like spring.

   ⓑ My mom likes spring.

   ⓒ I go on a picnic in the spring.

2

> *A:* I like fall and winter.
>
> *B:* _____
>
> *A:* I go sledding in the winter.

   ⓐ Who likes winter?

   ⓑ What season do you like?

   ⓒ What do you do in the winter?

Which of the following is true about the dialog?

> *Kate:* I like fall because the weather is good in the fall. It's not hot and it's not cold.
>
> *Ron:* You're right. It's a good season to go on a picnic.
>
> *Kate:* It's good for reading books, too.
>
> *Ron:* Do you like reading books?
>
> *Kate:* Yes. I read every day.

   ⓐ Kate likes reading books a lot.

   ⓑ Kate goes on a picnic in the fall.

   ⓒ Ron likes fall because of the fine weather.

Choose and write the correct phrase for the picture.

1

2

_____

_____

3

4

_____

_____

read a book   go on a picnic   swim in the swimming pool   go sledding

Fill in the blanks and complete the sentence.

1	2
3	4

1 I _____ in the spring.

2 I _____ in the swimming pool in the _____.

3 I _____ in the fall.

4 I _____ in the _____.

18

Unscramble and write the sentence.

1 seasons   do   like   what   ?   you

_____

2 fall   winter   and   like   I   .

_____

3 ?   do   do   you   fall   what   in   the

_____

4 picnic   I   a   go   .   in   the   on   fall

_____

Tick the unnecessary sentence and make a dialog.

____ What do you do in the summer?

____ What seasons do you like?

____ I like spring and summer.

____ I like spring better than summer.

____ I swim in the swimming pool.

_____

_____

_____

_____

I'm a Frog!

Choose and complete the cartoon.

go ice skating   go sledding   season   winter

What do you do in the winter?   What season do you like?

[1~4] Listen and write the number. T09

5 Listen and choose the correct picture. T10

ⓐ    ⓑ    ⓒ

[6~7] Listen and choose the correct answer. T11

6   ⓑ   ⓒ

7   ⓑ   ⓒ

22

[8~9] Choose the correct phrase.

8

She (reads a book /
goes sledding).

9

They (go on a picnic /
go ice skating).

10   Choose the best answer for the blank.

> *Sarah:* I like spring. I go on a picnic in the spring.
>   How about you?
> *Tom:* I like summer.
> _____

ⓐ I go sledding in the summer.
ⓑ My sister reads books in the summer.
ⓒ I swim in the swimming pool in the summer.

11   Fill in the blanks to complete the summary.

> *Sally:* What season do you like?
> *Jake:* I like fall. I can enjoy the fine weather.
> *Sally:* I like winter because I can go sledding.

Jake likes _____ because he _____, and

_____ likes _____ because she can go sledding.

Is Jane a Good Girl and Is Nick a Good Boy?

Quiz

Q: Do they get up early?

A: Yes. Nick gets up at 7 o'clock, _____ Jane gets up at 7 o'clock, too.

Quiz

Q: Do all of them sleep alone?

A: No. Jane sleeps alone, _____ Nick sleeps with his teddy bear.

■ Conjunction: and & but

접속사 and와 but은 두 문장을 연결하여 한 문장으로 만들 때 사용한다.
and는 두 문장의 내용이 비슷할 때, but은 두 문장의 내용이 반대일 때 사용한다.

I like cherries, and Katie likes cherries. 나는 체리를 좋아하고, Katie도 체리를 좋아한다.

Tom doesn't like Jane, and Jane doesn't like Tom.
Tom은 Jane을 좋아하지 않고, Jane도 Tom을 좋아하지 않는다.

I stay at home and (I) watch TV. 나는 집에 머물고 TV를 본다.

I like apples, but John doesn't like apples.
나는 사과를 좋아하지만, John은 사과를 좋아하지 않는다.

I have a book, but (I) don't read it. 나는 책을 한 권 가지고 있지만, 그것을 읽지 않는다.

Look at the picture and circle the correct word.

1

Kevin reads a book, (and / but)
Sarah reads a book.

2

I like ice cream, (and / but)
my dad doesn't like ice cream.

3

Bill plays baseball, (and / but)
Gloria doesn't play baseball.

4

I eat apples, (and / but) Sarah
eats apples.

Match the pairs to make a full sentence.

1 I love rock music,   but Tom has two cats.

2 Sarah has two dogs,   and my father likes classical music.

3 Mr. Brown can speak English,   but he can't read it.

Make the two sentences into one, using 'and' or 'but'.

1 I live in Korea. Tom lives in Korea.

_____

2 Tom reads books on Sundays. Tom watches TV on Sundays.

_____

3 Kevin likes Sarah. Sarah doesn't like Kevin.

_____

4 I want to call Jim. I don't have his phone number.

_____

Find the wrong part and rewrite the sentence correctly.

1 I have one sister but two brothers.

_____

2 Tom loves oranges, and I don't like oranges.

_____

3 My brother gets up early, and I get up late in the morning.

_____

4 Kevin stays at home but watches TV.

_____

■ Negative: don't & doesn't

일반동사의 부정형: don't [doesn't] + 동사원형

I like apples. → I don't like apples.

You have a brother → You don't have a brother.

We play the piano after 6 o'clock. → We don't play the piano after 6 o'clock.

They study hard. → They don't study hard.

He plays tennis. → He doesn't play tennis.

She reads books. → She doesn't read books.

Kevin likes carrots. → Kevin doesn't like carrots.

Look at the picture and circle the correct answer.

1

I (play / don't play) soccer
on Sundays.

2

They (go / don't go) on a picnic
in the winter.

3

Kevin (lives / doesn't live) in Korea.

4

She (likes / doesn't like) pizza.

Circle the correct answer.

1　I (don't / doesn't) watch TV after 9 o'clock.

2　We (don't / doesn't) play basketball.

3　She (don't / doesn't) like candies.

4　They (don't / doesn't) drink milk.

5　Kevin (don't / doesn't) play soccer on a rainy day.

Make negative sentence.

1　Sarah lives in America.

_____

2　I read a book at night.

_____

3　Tom and Kevin go ice skating in the winter.

_____

4　We like hamburgers.

_____

Unscramble and make a sentence.

1　don't　.　piano　the　play　I

_____

2　picnic　don't　like　on　go　they　a　.　to

_____

3　school　doesn't　Mike　go　to　Sundays　.　on

_____

A Free Ticket in the Golden Envelope 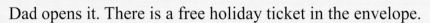 T12

Dad finds a golden envelope in the mailbox.

On the front, it says FREE TICKET.

Mom and Sarah shout, "Open it!"

Dad opens it. There is a free holiday ticket in the envelope.

"I hope it is to a beach," says Sarah. "I can swim
in the sea."

"No. I hope it is a camping holiday," says Dad. "I can
sleep in a tent _____ ⓐ _____ get fresh air."

"I want to go to a big city," says Mom. "I can go shopping
_____ ⓑ _____ go to the theater."

Then they start to argue. Beach! Camping! City! They argue on and on.

---

1 편지함 속에서 발견한 것이 무엇인지 고르세요.

① 무료 극장 티켓   ② 무료 캠핑 티켓   ③ 금빛 봉투

2 위 글의 빈칸 ⓐ와 ⓑ에 공통으로 들어갈 낱말을 고르세요.

① and   ② but   ③ for

3 위 글에 등장하는 인물들과 그들이 원하는 것을 바르게 연결하세요.

Then the phone rings. Sarah answers the phone.

"Hello, this is Lucky Holidays. You win a holiday to sunny Alexandria."

"Alexandria? My grandma lives there," says Sarah.

"This is Grandma!"

"Oh, Grandma, you tricked us!"

"I invite you all. Come and spend the holidays with me."

They go to Grandma's house and spend
two fun weeks.
Dad gets his fresh air. Mom goes shopping
and Sarah swims in the sea.
Everyone is happy.

4 위 글의 내용과 일치하지 않는 그림을 고르세요.

①    ②    ③

5 위 글의 내용으로 보아 금빛 봉투를 보낸 사람은 누구인가요?

① Sarah's friend.   ② Sarah's grandma.   ③ A tour company.

6 위 글의 내용과 일치하지 않는 것을 고르세요.

① Sarah's family invites her grandma.
② Sarah's grandma lives in Alexandria.
③ Sarah's family spends the holidays in Grandma's house.

Build up your word power.

⊙ golden

금빛의: bright yellow in color

Dad finds a _____ envelope in the mailbox.

⊙ envelope

봉투: a flat square paper container for a letter

On the front, the _____ says FREE TICKET.

⊙ free

무료의: without cost or payment

It says _____ TICKET.

⊙ shout

큰 소리로 말하다: to say something very loudly

Mom and Sarah _____, "Open it!"

⊙ holiday

휴일, 휴가: a time when you do not have to go to work or school

There is a free _____ ticket in the envelope.

⊙ camping

야영, 캠핑: staying in a tent for a holiday

I hope it is a _____ holiday.

⊙ **fresh**

신선한: cool or clean

I can sleep in a tent and get _____ air.

⊙ **shopping**

물건 사기, 쇼핑: the act of visiting shops to look at or buy goods

I can go _____ in a big city.

⊙ **argue**

논쟁하다: discuss something with others who have different opinions

They start to _____ .

⊙ **trick** 〔과거형: tricked〕

속이다: to deceive someone

Oh, Grandma, you _____ us!

⊙ **invite**

초대하다: to ask someone to come to your house, a party, or a meal

I _____ you all.

⊙ **spend**

(시간을) 보내다: to use time doing something

They go to Grandma's house and _____ two fun weeks.

1 Choose the common word for each blank.

> Kevin likes music, _____ he doesn't play the piano.
>
> I like Sarah, _____ she doesn't like me.

ⓐ and   ⓑ but   ⓒ or

2 Choose the wrong part and rewrite it correctly.

> I like fall <u>and</u> winter. I read books in the fall, <u>and</u> I don't go on a picnic.
>   ⓐ   ⓑ
> I go sledding <u>and</u> ice skating in the winter.
>   ⓒ

3 Choose the wrong sentence for the picture.

ⓐ The boy likes orange juice.
ⓑ The boy doesn't like bulgogi.
ⓒ The boy doesn't like hamburgers.

4 Choose the wrong sentence for the picture.

ⓐ Kevin and John play video games.
ⓑ Tom reads a book, but Sarah doesn't read a book.
ⓒ Mom plays the piano, but Dad doesn't play the piano.

5 Fill in the blank to complete the sentence for the picture.

I _____ hamburgers on my birthday.

I eat cake on my birthday.

[6~7] Read and choose the correct answers.

Today is Sunday.
I usually get up at 7 o'clock in the morning, but I got up at 10 o'clock
today. I _____ⓐ_____ go to school on Sundays.
My uncle, Billy, is a basketball player. He plays basketball on
weekdays, but he plays baseball with me on Sundays.
My mom _____ⓑ_____ go to work today. My mom and dad go to
church and go shopping together on Sundays. My dad is a teacher, but
he doesn't teach his students on Sundays. He teaches me!

6 Which of the following is suitable for the blanks ⓐ and ⓑ?

ⓐ don't – doesn't
ⓑ don't – don't
ⓒ doesn't – doesn't

7 Which of the following does NOT happen on Sundays?

ⓐ 　　ⓑ 　　ⓒ

Listen and repeat the dialog. ○ T13

When is your birthday?

My birthday is on Children's Day.

Really?
My birthday is on Children's Day, too.

What do you want for a present?

I want a game CD. What about you?

I want a cell phone.

Speak aloud. ○ T14

1
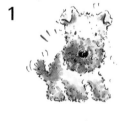
pet

2

computer

3

in-line skates

Listen and choose the correct picture. 🔘 T15

1 ⓐ  ⓑ  ⓒ

2 ⓐ  ⓑ  ⓒ

Listen and choose the correct answer. 🔘 T16

1 *A:* _____

B: My birthday is on Christmas Day.

2 *A:* _____

B: I want a ball.

Listen and choose the correct dialog. 🔘 T17

Listen and repeat the words. T18

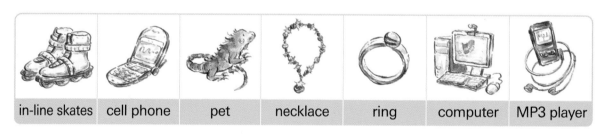

| in-line skates | cell phone | pet | necklace | ring | computer | MP3 player |

Listen and choose the correct picture. T19

1 ⓐ ⓑ   2 ⓐ ⓑ

Choose the correct word for the picture.

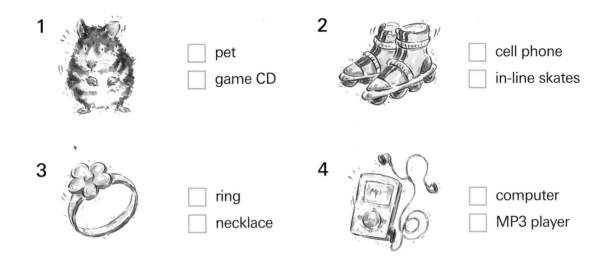

1 ☐ pet
   ☐ game CD

2 ☐ cell phone
   ☐ in-line skates

3 ☐ ring
   ☐ necklace

4 ☐ computer
   ☐ MP3 player

Connect the matching pairs and fill in the blanks.

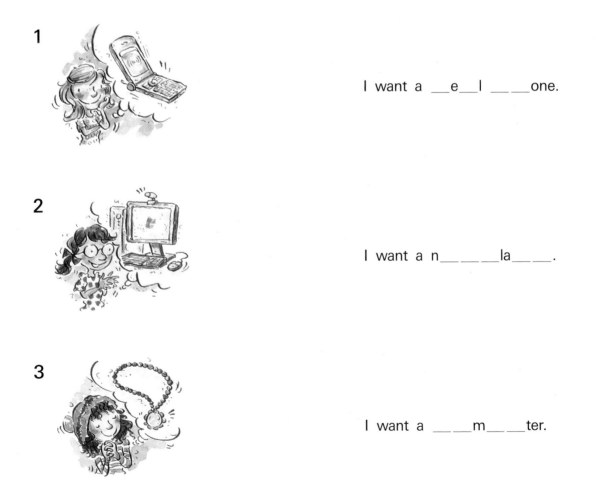

1 I want a __e__l __ __one.

2 I want a n__ __ __ __la__ __ __.

3 I want a __ __m__ __ter.

Match to make a dialog.

1 (When is your birthday?)   (I want a game CD.)

2 (What do you want for
a present?)   (My birthday is on
Children's Day.)

Read the sentence and write the correct answer.

ⓐ    ⓑ

ⓒ    ⓓ

1 ____ My birthday is on Christmas Day. I want a cell phone.

2 ____ My birthday is on Children's Day. I want in-line skates.

3 ____ My birthday is on April 5th. I want a computer.

4 ____ My birthday is on March 2nd. I want a pet.

⊛ *CHALLENGE!*

Choose the correct answer.

1

> A: _____
>
> B: I want an MP3 player.

   ⓐ What do you like to do?

   ⓑ What do you have in your hand?

   ⓒ What do you want for a present?

2

> A: When is your birthday?
>
> B: I was born on Children's Day.
>
> A: Really? Then your birthday is _____ .

   ⓐ May 1st

   ⓑ May 5th

   ⓒ May 8th

3

> A: Min-su, when is your birthday?
>
> B: My birthday is in one week.
>
> A: What's the date today?
>
> B: Today is May 3rd.
>
> A: Aha! Then your birthday is _____ .

   ⓐ May 3rd

   ⓑ May 4th

   ⓒ May 10th

Look at the picture and fill in the blanks.

My name is Joyce.

I like winter.

In the winter, I can make snowmen.

I can have _____.

And I have my birthday!

My birthday is on _____.

I want a _____ for a present.

Children's Day   cell phone   Christmas Day   computer   snow fights

Complete the dialog for the picture.

1

A: When is your birthday?

B: _____

2

A: What do you want for a present?

B: _____

Unscramble and write the sentence.

1   your   when   is   ?   birthday

_____

2   birthday   Christmas Day   is   my   on   .

_____

3   what   want   do   a present   for   you   ?

_____

4   a bike   I   for   want   a present   .

_____

Tick the unnecessary sentence and make a dialog.

____ What do you want for a present?

____ When is your birthday?

____ I want a CD player for a present.

____ I am 12 years old.

____ My birthday is on Children's Day.

_____

_____

_____

_____

This Is for You

Choose and complete the cartoon.

on Christmas Day   Thank you!   When is your birthday?   winter

[1~6] Listen and write the number. T20

7 Listen and choose the correct picture. T21

ⓐ  ⓑ  ⓒ

[8~9] Listen and choose the correct answer. T22

8   ⓑ   ⓒ

9   ⓑ   ⓒ

[10~12] Write the word for the picture.

| cell phone | MP3 player | necklace | ring | computer |

10

_____

11

_____

12

_____

[13~14] Choose the correct answer for the blank.

13

> *Cathy:* What's that, Mike?
> *Mike:* It's a notebook computer. Do you have one?
> *Cathy:* Not now, but my dad will buy one for a birthday present.
> *Mike:* Really? _____
> *Cathy:* My birthday is on Children's Day.

ⓐ What is your birthday?
ⓑ When is your birthday?
ⓒ How is your birthday?

14

> *Dad:* Sue, this Sunday is your birthday.
>   What do you want for a present?
> *Sue:* Hmm.... _____
> *Dad:* Puppy or kitty?
> *Sue:* Puppy will be great!

ⓐ I want a pet.   ⓑ I want a game CD.   ⓒ I want a puppy.

When Is Your Birthday?

Quiz

Q: _____ is Jeff's birthday?

A: His birthday is on _____.

Quiz Q: _____ does Amy want for a present?

A: She wants a game CD.

■ Question Word: When

When + Verb	When is your birthday? 너의 생일은 언제니? When do you go to school? 너는 언제 학교에 가니? When can you come? 너는 언제 올 수 있니? When will you finish work? 너는 언제 일을 끝낼 거니?

Write the correct question word.

1

A: _____ is your birthday?

B: My birthday is May 1st.

2

A: _____ do you go to school?

B: I go to school at 8 o'clock.

3

A: _____ can you come?

B: I can come by tomorrow.

4

A: _____ will you finish
your homework?

B: I will finish it after dinner.

Match the pairs to make a dialog.

1
When is your birthday?

I go to school at 8 o'clock.

2
When do you go to school?

I can come by 5 o'clock.

3
When can you come to my farm?

My birthday is April 5th.

Unscramble and write the sentence.

1   your   when   birthday   is   ?

_____

2   birthday   my   May 1st   is   .

_____

3   can   you   come   when   ?

_____

4   by   will   6 o'clock   come   I   .

_____

■ Prepositions of Time: on & at

on + 요일, 특정한 날 (때)	I'll visit my grandparents on Sunday. 나는 일요일에 할아버지, 할머니 댁에 갈 것이다. My birthday is on New Year's Day. 내 생일은 설날이다. I usually go swimming on weekends. 나는 대개 주말마다 수영하러 간다.
at + 시각	I get up at 7 o'clock. 나는 7시에 일어난다. We have lunch at noon. 우리는 12시 (정오)에 점심을 먹는다. The birds don't sleep at night. 그 새들은 밤에 잠을 자지 않는다.

Write the correct preposition.

1

A: What will you do this Sunday?

B: I'll go to the zoo _____ Sunday.

2

A: When is your birthday?

B: My birthday is _____ Children's Day.

3

A: What time do you have lunch?

B: I have lunch _____ noon.

4

A: What time do you go to bed?

B: I go to bed _____ 11 o'clock.

Choose and complete the sentence.

> Christmas Day   New Year's Day   Arbor Day   Children's Day

1 My birthday is January 1st.

→ My birthday is on _____.

2 My birthday is April 5th.

→ My birthday is on _____.

3 My birthday is May 5th.

→ My birthday is on _____.

4 My birthday is December 25th.

→ My birthday is on _____.

There are two mistakes in the sentences. Correct the mistakes.

What Is Your Birth Symbol? 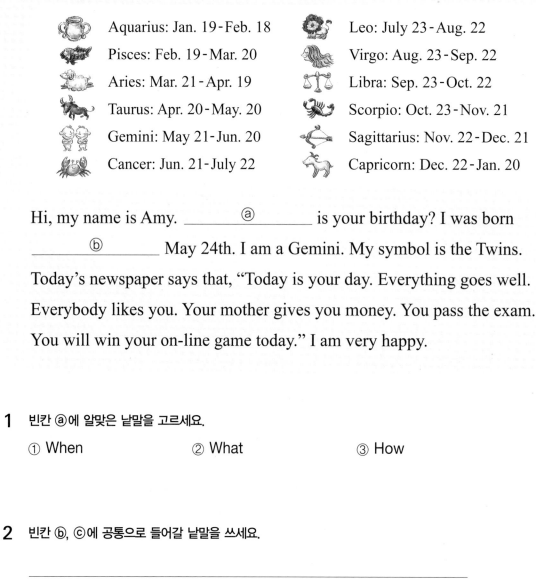 T23

Aquarius: Jan. 19-Feb. 18		Leo: July 23-Aug. 22	
Pisces: Feb. 19-Mar. 20		Virgo: Aug. 23-Sep. 22	
Aries: Mar. 21-Apr. 19		Libra: Sep. 23-Oct. 22	
Taurus: Apr. 20-May. 20		Scorpio: Oct. 23-Nov. 21	
Gemini: May 21-Jun. 20		Sagittarius: Nov. 22-Dec. 21	
Cancer: Jun. 21-July 22		Capricorn: Dec. 22-Jan. 20	

Hi, my name is Amy. _____ⓐ_____ is your birthday? I was born _____ⓑ_____ May 24th. I am a Gemini. My symbol is the Twins. Today's newspaper says that, "Today is your day. Everything goes well. Everybody likes you. Your mother gives you money. You pass the exam. You will win your on-line game today." I am very happy.

1 빈칸 ⓐ에 알맞은 낱말을 고르세요.

① When   ② What   ③ How

2 빈칸 ⓑ, ⓒ에 공통으로 들어갈 낱말을 쓰세요.

_____

3 다음 그림 중 Amy에게 일어날 일이 아닌 것을 고르세요.

My best friend, Julie was born _____©_____ August 17th.

She is a Leo. Her symbol is _____ⓓ_____. Today is bad for Leos.

It says, "Be careful of cars and water. Do not play soccer or basketball.

You will get hurt. After school, you should stay

in your room."

Poor Julie! She must stay home today.

Do you know your symbol?

Find yours.

It's fun!

---

4 빈칸 ⓓ에 알맞은 것을 고르세요.

① the Fish
② the Lion
③ the Lady

5 위 글의 내용과 일치하지 않는 것을 고르세요.

① Julie is a Leo.
② Today is bad for Leos.
③ Julie got hurt today.

6 여러분 자신의 생일과 별자리를 쓰세요.

_____

Build up your word power.

⊙ symbol

상징: a thing that shows something

The dove is the _____ of peace.

⊙ twins

쌍둥이: two people that are born at the same time and have
        the same mother

Jerry and Jamie are _____.

⊙ newspaper

신문: a daily or weekly paper

I like to read the _____.

⊙ money

돈: coins or banknotes used as a means of buying things

Your mother gives you _____.

⊙ exam

시험: a set of tasks, especially in written form, designed to test
        knowledge or ability

You pass the _____.

⊙ win

이기다: to be victorious or come first in

You'll _____ your on-line game today.

⊙ best

가장 좋은: favorite

My ＿＿＿＿＿＿＿ friend is Julie.

⊙ careful

조심하는: taking care to avoid harm or damage

Be ＿＿＿＿＿＿＿ of cars.

⊙ basketball

농구: a game in which two teams of five players score by throwing a ball into a net

Do not play ＿＿＿＿＿＿＿.

⊙ hurt

다친: suffering pain or injury

You will get ＿＿＿＿＿＿＿.

⊙ poor

불쌍한: expressing pity or sympathy

How ＿＿＿＿＿＿＿ he is!

⊙ find

찾다: to discover

I must ＿＿＿＿＿＿＿ the key.

1 Choose the common word for each blank.

> _____ do you go to school?
>
> _____ do you get up?

ⓐ When ⓑ What ⓒ Who

2 Choose the sentence that doesn't fit the blank.

> *A:* When is your birthday?
>
> *B:* _____

ⓐ Today is Children's Day.
ⓑ My birthday is May 5th.
ⓒ Tomorrow is my birthday.

3 When is Kate's birthday? Choose the correct answer.

Her birthday is _____.

ⓐ May 5th
ⓑ March 5th
ⓒ April 5th

4 Choose the common preposition for each blank.

> My birthday is _____ New Year's Day.
>
> I'll go to the movies _____ Sunday.

ⓐ in ⓑ on ⓒ at

5 Read and fill in the blank.

> Hi, my name is Tom.
>
> Guess when my birthday is.
>
> I was born two days before Christmas.

Tom's birthday is _____.

[6~7] Read and choose the correct answers.

> *Mike:* Su-jin, what a nice cell phone!
>
> *Su-jin:* My dad gave it to me for a birthday present.
>
> *Mike:* Wow! Great! When was your birthday?
>
> *Su-jin:* It was yesterday.
>
> *Mike:* Congrats! I want to give you a present.
>   What do you want?
>
> *Su-jin:* Hmm, I want a teddy bear.
>
> *Mike:* OK.

6 Who gave Su-jin a cell phone?

ⓐ Su-jin's dad.
ⓑ Su-jin's mom.
ⓒ Mike.

7 What will Su-jin receive as a birthday present from Mike?

ⓐ A cell phone.
ⓑ An MP3 player.
ⓒ A teddy bear.

Roller coaster

Roller Coaster E2
Student Book

UNIT 01

P. 13

 1 I like summer.
2 I swim in the swimming pool.

1 ⓑ   2 ⓒ

 1 ⓐ What seasons do you like?
ⓑ Do you swim in the summer?
ⓒ What do you do in the summer?
2 ⓐ I like summer better.
ⓑ I go on a picnic in the spring.
ⓒ I go ice skating in the winter.

1 ⓐ   2 ⓑ

 ⓐ A: What do you do in the summer?
B: I like spring and summer.
ⓑ A: What seasons do you like?
B: I like to go on a picnic.
ⓒ A: What do you do in the fall?
B: I read books in the fall.

ⓒ

P. 14

 1 winter   2 read a book

1 ⓑ   2 ⓐ

P. 15

1 ⓔ   2 ⓒ   3 ⓐ

1 I r e a d books in the s p ring.
2 I s w im in the swimming p o o l in the s u m m e r.
3 I go o n a pic n ic in the f a ll.
4 I g o ice s k ating in the w int e r.

P. 16

1 ⓐ   2 ⓑ   3 ⓒ   4 ⓑ

1 (What seasons do you like?) (I go on a picnic.)
2 (What do you do in the spring?) (I like spring and summer.)

P. 17

1 ⓐ   2 ⓒ

ⓐ

P. 18

1 go on a picnic   2 swim in the swimming pool
3 go sledding   4 read a book

1 read a book   2 swim, summer
3 go on a picnic   4 go sledding, winter

P. 19

1 What seasons do you like?
2 I like fall and winter.
3 What do you do in the fall?
4 I go on a picnic in the fall.

____ What do you do in the summer?
____ What seasons do you like?
____ I like spring and summer.
✓ I like spring better than summer.
____ I swim in the swimming pool.

What seasons do you like?
I like spring and summer.
What do you do in the summer?
I swim in the swimming pool.

P. 20-21

CARTOON

What <u>season</u> do you like, Sarah?
I like <u>winter</u>.
What do you do in the winter?
What season do you like?
Do you <u>go ice skating</u>?
Do you <u>go sledding</u> in the winter?

P. 22-23

TEST

 1 winter   2 summer   3 fall   4 spring

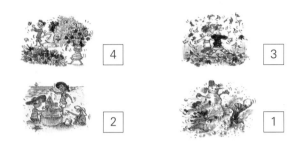

🎧 5 I go on a picnic.

ⓒ

🎧 6 Q: What seasons do you like?
   ⓐ I go ice skating in the winter.
   ⓑ I like spring and summer.
   ⓒ Korea has four seasons.
7 Q: What do you do in the spring?
   ⓐ I swim in the swimming pool in the summer.
   ⓑ Spring is a beautiful season.
   ⓒ I go on a picnic in the spring.

6 ⓑ   7 ⓒ
8 reads a book   9 go ice skating   10 ⓒ
11 fall, can enjoy the fine weather, Sally, winter

UNIT 02

P. 24-25

CARTOON

Quiz	Q: Do they get up early?
	A: Yes. Nick gets up at 7 o'clock, __and__ Jane gets up at 7 o'clock, too.

Quiz	Q: Do all of them sleep alone?
	A: No. Jane sleeps alone, __but__ Nick sleeps with his teddy bear.

P. 26

1 and   2 but   3 but   4 and

P. 27

1 I love rock music,   but Tom has two cats.
2 Sarah has two dogs,   and my father likes classical music.
3 Mr. Brown can speak English, —— but he can't read it.

1 I live in Korea, and Tom lives in Korea.
2 Tom reads books and watches TV on Sundays.
3 Kevin likes Sarah, but Sarah doesn't like Kevin.
4 I want to call Jim, but I don't have his phone number.

1 I have one sister and two brothers.
2 Tom loves oranges, but I don't like oranges.
3 My brother gets up early, but I get up late in the morning.
4 Kevin stays at home and watches TV.

P. 28

1 play   2 don't go
3 doesn't live   4 likes

P. 29

1 don't   2 don't   3 doesn't
4 don't   5 doesn't

1 Sarah doesn't live in America.
2 I don't read a book at night.
3 Tom and Kevin don't go ice skating in the winter.
4 We don't like hamburgers.

1 I don't play the piano.
2 They don't like to go on a picnic.
3 Mike doesn't go to school on Sundays.

P. 30-31

금빛 봉투 속의 무료 티켓
아빠가 우편함에서 금빛 봉투를 발견해요. 봉투 앞에는 '무료 티켓'이 라고 쓰여 있어요. 엄마와 사라가 소리쳐요. "열어 보세요!" 아빠가 열 어 봐요. 봉투 안에는 무료 휴가 티켓이 들어 있어요. "바닷가로 가는 거면 좋겠어요." 사라가 말해요. "바다에서 수영할 수 있잖아요." "아 니, 나는 캠핑 휴가였으면 좋겠어," 아빠가 말해요. "텐트에서 자고 신 선한 공기도 쐴 수 있잖아." "난 대도시로 가고 싶어요," 엄마가 말해 요. "쇼핑도 하고 극장에도 갈 수 있잖아요." 그들은 논쟁하기 시작해 요. 바닷가! 캠핑! 도시! 그들은 계속해서 논쟁해요.
그 때 전화벨이 울려요. 사라가 전화를 받아요.
"여보세요, 행운의 휴가입니다. 당신은 화창한 알렉산드리아행 휴가에

당첨되셨습니다." "알렉산드리아? 거기는 우리 할머니가 사시는데."
사라가 말해요. "내가 할머니란다!" "이런, 할머니! 우릴 속이셨군요!"
"너희 모두를 초대하마. 와서 나와 함께 휴가를 보내자꾸나."
그들은 할머니댁으로 가서 신나는 두 주를 보내요. 아빠는 신선한 공기
를 마셔요. 엄마는 쇼핑하러 가고 사라는 바다에서 헤엄쳐요. 모두가
행복해요.

1 ③　　　　2 ①
3
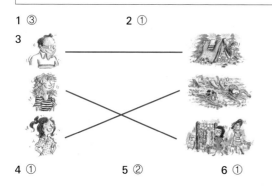
4 ①　　　5 ②　　　6 ①

P. 32-33

golden / envelope / FREE / shout / holiday / camping /
fresh / shopping / argue / tricked / invite / spend

P. 34-35

TEST

1 ⓑ　　2 ⓑ　　3 ⓑ　　4 ⓒ
5 don't eat　6 ⓐ　　7 ⓐ

UNIT 03

P. 37

 1 My birthday is on Children's Day.
2 I want a computer.

1 ⓐ　　　　2 ⓑ

 1 ⓐ What's the date today?
　ⓑ When is your birthday?
　ⓒ When is your mom's birthday?
2 ⓐ What do you like?
　ⓑ What can you see?
　ⓒ What do you want for a present?

1 ⓑ　　　　2 ⓒ

 ⓐ A: What day is it?
　　B: My birthday is on Children's Day.
ⓑ A: What do you want for a present?
　　B: I want a game CD.
ⓒ A: When is your birthday?
　　B: It's Monday today.

ⓑ

P. 38

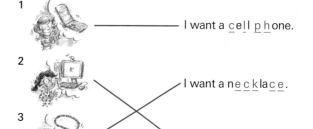 1 in-line skates　　　2 ring

1 ⓐ　　　　2 ⓑ

P. 39

1 pet　　　　　2 in-line skates
3 ring　　　　4 MP3 player

1

I want a c e l l   p h one.
I want a n e c k l a c e.
I want a c o m p u ter.

P. 40

1
2
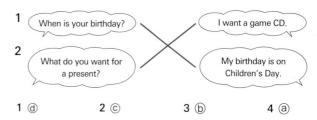
1 ⓓ　　2 ⓒ　　3 ⓑ　　4 ⓐ

P. 41

1 ⓒ　　　　2 ⓑ　　　　3 ⓒ

P. 42

snow fights, Christmas Day, computer

1 *A:* When is your birthday?

   B: My birthday is on Christmas Day.

     [My birthday is December 25th.]

2 *A:* What do you want for a present?

   B: I want a cell phone.

P. 43

1 When is your birthday?

2 My birthday is on Christmas Day.

3 What do you want for a present?

4 I want a bike for a present.

___ What do you want for a present?

___ When is your birthday?

___ I want a CD player for a present.

✓ I am 12 years old.

___ My birthday is on Children's Day.

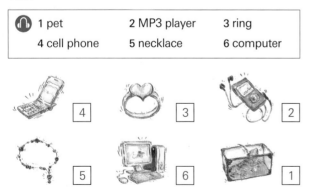 When is your birthday?

My birthday is on Children's Day.

What do you want for a present?

I want a CD player for a present.

P. 44-45

CARTOON

Well, Clara. When is your birthday?

My birthday is <u>on Christmas Day</u>.

<u>Thank you!</u>

I will wear these in the <u>winter</u>.

P. 46-47

TEST

1 pet	2 MP3 player	3 ring
4 cell phone	5 necklace	6 computer

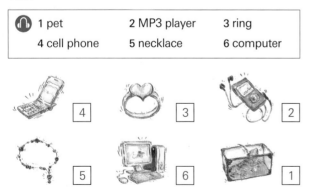

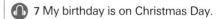 7 My birthday is on Christmas Day.

ⓑ

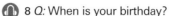 8 *Q:* When is your birthday?

   ⓐ My birthday is on Children's Day.

   ⓑ I like my birthday.

   ⓒ I want a game CD.

9 *Q:* What do you want for a present?

   ⓐ My birthday is on Christmas.

   ⓑ No, I want.

   ⓒ I want a pet.

8 ⓐ   9 ⓒ

10 cell phone   11 necklace   12 computer

13 ⓑ   14 ⓐ

UNIT 04

P. 48-49

CARTOON

Quiz	*Q:* <u> When </u> is Jeff's birthday?
	A: His birthday is on <u> Children's Day </u>.

Quiz	*Q:* <u> What </u> does Amy want for a present?
	A: She wants a game CD.

P. 50

1 When   2 When   3 When   4 When

P. 51

1

2

3

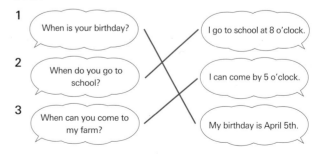

1 When is your birthday?
2 My birthday is May 1st.
3 When can you come?
4 I will come by 6 o'clock.

P. 52

1 on   2 on   3 at   4 at

P. 53

1 New Year's Day   2 Arbor Day
3 Children's Day   4 Christmas Day

My birthday is ~~at~~ Children's Day. → on
Today is my birthday. I'm going to have a party ~~on~~ 7 o'clock.
→ at

P. 54-55

네 탄생 상징은 무엇이니?

물병자리 1.19–2.18	사자자리 7. 23–8.22
물고기자리 2.19–3.20	처녀자리 8.23–9.22
양자리 3.21–4.19	천칭자리 9.23–10.22
황소자리 4.20–5.20	전갈자리 10.23–11.21
쌍둥이자리 5.21–6.20	사수자리 11.22–12.21
게자리 6.21–7. 22	염소자리 12.22–1.20

안녕, 내 이름은 에이미야. 네 생일은 언제니? 나는 5월 24일에 태어났어. 나는 쌍둥이자리야. 내 상징은 쌍둥이야.
오늘 신문에 쓰여 있기를, "오늘은 당신의 날입니다. 모든 게 잘 됩니다. 모두가 당신을 좋아합니다. 어머니가 당신에게 돈을 주실 것입니다. 시험에 통과할 것입니다. 온라인 게임에도 이길 겁니다." 나는 아주 행복해.

나의 가장 좋은 친구, 줄리는 8월 17일에 태어났어. 줄리는 사자자리야. 그녀의 상징은 사자야. 오늘은 사자자리에게 좋지 않아. 신문에 쓰여 있기를, "자동차와 물을 조심하세요. 축구나 농구를 하지 마세요. 다칠 수 있습니다. 방과 후에는 방 안에만 있어야 합니다." 불쌍한 줄리! 그녀는 오늘 집에 있어야만 해. 너는 네 상징을 아니? 네 상징을 찾아 봐. 재미있어!

1 ①   2 on   3 ②
4 ②   5 ③

P. 56-57

symbol / twins / newspaper / money / exam / win / best / careful / basketball / hurt / poor / find

P. 58-59

TEST

1 ⓐ   2 ⓐ   3 ⓐ   4 ⓑ
5 December 23rd   6 ⓐ   7 ⓒ

Roller Coaster E2

Workbook & Test

UNIT 01

P. 2

B

1 가을 — fall
2 여름 — summer
3 겨울 — spring
4 봄 — winter
5 소풍 가다 — go on a picnic
6 책을 읽다 — read a book
7 수영장에서 수영하다 — swim in the swimming pool

P. 5

D

1   summer
2   winter
3   go on a picnic
4   read a book
5   spring
6   fall
7   go ice skating

E

Ⅰ ①What seasons do you like?
I like ②spring and fall.
What do you do ③in the fall?
④I read books.

Ⅱ I like spring.
⑤I go on a picnic in the spring.
How about you?
I like summer.
⑥I swim in the swimming pool in the summer.

UNIT 02

P. 7

B

a	s	h	i	n	v	i	t	e
r	k	b	u	p	t	n	k	n
f	r	e	s	h	o	v	f	v
b	g	o	l	d	e	n	v	e
b	u	e	r	c	h	l	g	l
u	t	a	s	h	o	u	t	o
t	d	f	r	e	e	r	e	p
t	r	i	n	d	f	i	e	e
r	h	o	l	i	d	a	y	o

1 무료의   free
2 신선한   fresh
3 초대하다   invite
4 봉투   envelope
5 금빛의   golden
6 큰 소리로 말하다   shout
7 휴일, 휴가   holiday
8 그러나   but

P. 8

C 1 and   2 but   3 but

D 1 I stay at home and watch TV.
2 I help Mom, and he helps Dad.
3 I like apples, but Kate doesn't like apples.

P. 9

E   1 don't   2 doesn't   3 don't

F   1 I don't live in Korea.
     2 She doesn't drink milk.
     3 They don't go on a picnic in the winter.

P. 10

G

     1 _____ golden _____
     2 _____ holiday _____
     3 _____ fresh _____
     4 _____ envelope _____
     5 _____ free _____
     6 _____ trick _____
     7 _____ invite _____

H

     1 They _don't_ go on a picnic in the winter.
     2 Tom reads books _and_ watches TV _on_ Sundays.
     3 I like apples, but John _doesn't like apples_ .
     4 They find a _golden envelope_ in the mailbox.
     5 There is a _free holiday ticket_ in the envelope.
     6 I can sleep in a tent and get _fresh_ air.

UNIT 03

P. 12

B

1 cell phone   2 computer   3 pet
4 present   5 necklace   6 birthday
7 ring

P. 15

D

     1 _____ pet _____
     2 _____ necklace _____
     3 _____ computer _____
     4 _____ in-line skates _____
     5 _____ ring _____
     6 _____ cell phone _____
     7 _____ MP3 player _____

E

I   ①When is your birthday?
     My birthday is ②on Christmas Day.
     What do you want ③for a present?
     ④I want a computer.

II   My birthday is in one week.
     ⑤What's the date today?
     Today is ⑥May 3rd.
     Then ⑦your birthday is May 10th.

UNIT 04

P. 17

B

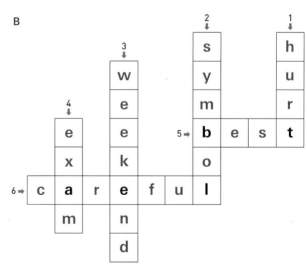

67

1 다친	hurt	
2 상징	symbol	
3 주말	weekend	
4 시험	exam	
5 가장 좋은	best	
6 조심하는	careful	

P. 18

C   1 When   2 When   3 When

D   1 When can you come?
      2 When do you get up?
      3 When will you go sledding?

P. 19

E   1 on   2 on   3 at

F   1 I play basketball on weekends.
      2 She'll have a party at 7 o'clock.
      3 The bird doesn't sleep at night.

P. 20

G

    1 weekend
    2 symbol
    3 baseball
    4 special
    5 best
    6 careful
    7 twins

H

    1 When will you do your homework?
    2 My birthday is on Children's Day.
    3 I usually go to school at 8 o'clock.
    4 I like to read the newspaper.
    5 Be careful of cars and water.
    6 Do not play soccer or basketball.

Achievement Test

 1 swim in the swimming pool
     2 go on a picnic

1 ⓐ   2 ⓑ

3 ⓐ I go sledding in the winter.
    ⓑ I go ice skating in the winter.
    ⓒ I go ice skating in the fall.
4 ⓐ A: What do you do in the winter?
      B: I go ice skating in the winter.
   ⓑ A: What season do you like?
      B: I like summer.
   ⓒ A: What do you do in the spring?
      B: I read books in the spring.

3 ⓑ	4 ⓒ	
5 ⓑ	6 ⓒ	7 ⓒ
8 ⓐ	9 ⓐ	

10 Kate doesn't like cats, but she likes dogs.

11 ⓑ	12 ⓑ

Final Test

 1 ⓐ ring   ⓑ fat   ⓒ pet
     2 ⓐ computer   ⓑ cell phone   ⓒ MP3 player

1 ⓒ   2 ⓑ

3 ⓐ My birthday is on Children's Day.
    ⓑ I want a game CD.
    ⓒ I want in-line skates.

ⓑ

4 Q: When is your birthday?
   ⓐ My birthday is on April 5th.
   ⓑ I want a necklace.
   ⓒ No, I don't.

ⓐ

5 ⓐ	6 ⓒ	7 ⓒ
8 ⓑ	9 ⓐ	10 ⓑ
11 ⓒ	12 ⓑ	

01 What Seasons Do You Like?

A Write and say aloud.

1	계절	season
2	봄	spring
3	여름	summer
4	가을	fall
5	겨울	winter
6	소풍 가다	go on a picnic
7	책을 읽다	read a book
8	썰매 타러 가다	go sledding
9	스케이트 타러 가다	go ice skating
10	수영장에서 수영하다	swim in the swimming pool

B Match and fill in the blanks.

c	l	g	b	m	p	r

1 가을   •   • su___me___

2 여름   •   • fal___

3 겨울   •   • s___rin___

4 봄   •   • winte___

5 소풍 가다   •   • ___ead a ___ook

6 책을 읽다   •   • ___o on a ___i___nic

7 수영장에서 수영하다   •   • swi___ in
the swi___ming ___ool

C Write and say aloud.

1 너는 어떤 계절들을 좋아하니?

   What seasons do you like?

2 난 가을과 겨울이 좋아.

   I like fall and winter.

3 나도 겨울을 좋아해.

   I like winter, too.

4 난 겨울에 눈사람을 만들고 눈싸움을 하면서 놀아.

   I make snowmen and enjoy snow fights in the winter.

5 넌 겨울에 무엇을 하니?

   What do you do in the winter?

6 난 썰매를 타러 가.

I go sledding.

7 난 봄에 책을 읽어.

I read books in the spring.

8 난 여름에 수영장에서 수영을 해.

I swim in the swimming pool in the summer.

9 난 가을에 소풍을 가.

I go on a picnic in the fall.

10 난 겨울에 스케이트를 타러 가.

I go ice skating in the winter.

4

D Listen and write the word. 🎧 T24

1. _____

2. _____

3. _____

4. _____

5. _____

6. _____

7. _____

E Listen and fill in the blanks. 🎧 T25

I ① _____ do you like?

I like ② _____ .

What do you do ③ _____ ?

④ _____ .

II I like spring.

⑤ _____ .

How about you?

I like summer.

⑥ _____ .

02 Is Jane a Good Girl and Is Nick a Good Boy?

A Write and say aloud.

1	그리고	and
2	그러나	but
3	금빛의	golden
4	봉투	envelope
5	무료의	free
6	큰 소리로 말하다	shout
7	휴일, 휴가	holiday
8	야영, 캠핑	camping
9	신선한	fresh
10	논쟁하다	argue
11	속이다	trick
12	초대하다	invite

B Find, circle and write the word.

a	s	h	i	n	v	i	t	e
r	k	b	u	p	t	n	k	n
f	r	e	s	h	o	v	f	v
b	g	o	l	d	e	n	v	e
b	u	e	r	c	h	l	g	l
u	t	a	s	h	o	u	t	o
t	d	f	r	e	e	r	e	p
t	r	i	n	d	f	i	e	e
r	h	o	l	i	d	a	y	o

1 무료의 _____

2 신선한 _____

3 초대하다 _____

4 봉투 _____

5 금빛의 _____

6 큰 소리로 말하다 _____

7 휴일, 휴가 _____

8 그러나 _____

C Fill in the blank.

1 나는 축구를 좋아하고, 내 남동생도 축구를 좋아한다.

I like soccer, _____ my brother likes soccer.

2 Tom은 일찍 일어나지만, Jane은 일찍 일어나지 않는다.

Tom gets up early, _____ Jane doesn't get up early.

3 Kevin은 야구를 하지만, Sarah는 야구를 하지 않는다.

Kevin plays baseball, _____ Sarah doesn't play baseball.

D Unscramble the words to make a sentence.

1 나는 집에 머물고 TV를 본다.

| at | stay | I | home | TV | watch | and |

_____ .

2 나는 엄마를 돕고, 그는 아빠를 돕는다.

| help | I | Mom | and | , | helps | he | Dad |

_____ .

3 나는 사과를 좋아하지만, Kate는 사과를 좋아하지 않는다.

| but | I | apples | like | doesn't | apples | Kate | , | like |

_____ .

8

E Fill in the blank.

1 나는 햄버거를 좋아하지 않는다.

   I _____ like hamburgers.

2 John은 열심히 공부하지 않는다.

   John _____ study hard.

3 우리는 일요일마다 학교에 가지 않는다.

   We _____ go to school on Sundays.

F Unscramble the words to make a sentence.

1 나는 한국에 살지 않는다.

   | don't | I | in | Korea | live |

   _____.

2 그녀는 우유를 마시지 않는다.

   | doesn't | she | milk | drink |

   _____.

3 그들은 겨울에는 소풍을 가지 않는다.

   | a picnic | don't | in | they | winter | on | the | go |

   _____.

Listen and write the word. 🎧 T26

1 _____

2 _____

3 _____

4 _____

5 _____

6 _____

7 _____

H **Listen and fill in the blanks.** 🎧 T27

1 They _____ go on a picnic in the winter.

2 Tom reads books _____ watches TV _____ Sundays.

3 I like apples, but John _____ .

4 They find a _____ in the mailbox.

5 There is a _____ in the envelope.

6 I can sleep in a tent and get _____ air.

03 My Birthday Is on Children's Day

A Write and say aloud.

1	생일	birthday
2	선물	present
3	게임 CD	game CD
4	인라인 스케이트	in-line skates
5	휴대 전화	cell phone
6	애완동물	pet
7	목걸이	necklace
8	반지	ring
9	컴퓨터	computer
10	MP3 플레이어	MP3 player

Unscramble and write the word.

1 휴대 전화   e n p l   c l o h e   _____

2 컴퓨터   e t o p   u r m c   _____

3 애완동물   e t p   _____

4 선물   r e s   t p n e   _____

5 목걸이   k e l a   e n c c   _____

6 생일   h y i r   t d b a   _____

7 반지   g n i r   _____

C Write and say aloud.

1 네 생일은 언제니?

When is your birthday?

2 내 생일은 어린이날이야.

My birthday is on Children's Day.

3 내 생일도 어린이날이야.

My birthday is on Children's Day, too.

4 너는 선물로 무엇을 원하니?

What do you want for a present?

5 나는 게임 CD를 원해.

I want a game CD.

6 넌 어때?

What about you?

7 난 휴대 전화를 원해.

I want a cell phone.

8 내 생일은 크리스마스야.

My birthday is on Christmas Day.

9 난 어린이날에 태어났어.

I was born on Children's Day.

10 내 생일은 4월 5일이야.

My birthday is on April 5th.

D Listen and write the word. 🎧 T28

1 _____

2 _____

3 _____

4 _____

5 _____

6 _____

7 _____

E Listen and fill in the blanks. 🎧 T29

I ① _____ your birthday?

My birthday is ② _____ .

What do you want ③ _____ ?

④ _____ .

II My birthday is in one week.

⑤ _____ ?

Today is ⑥ _____ .

Then ⑦ _____ .

04 When Is Your Birthday?

A Write and say aloud.

1	특별한	special
2	크리스마스	Christmas
3	설날	New Year's Day
4	주말	weekend
5	상징	symbol
6	쌍둥이	twins
7	시험	exam
8	신문	newspaper
9	농구	basketball
10	다친	hurt
11	가장 좋은	best
12	조심하는	careful

B Do the crossword puzzle and write the words.

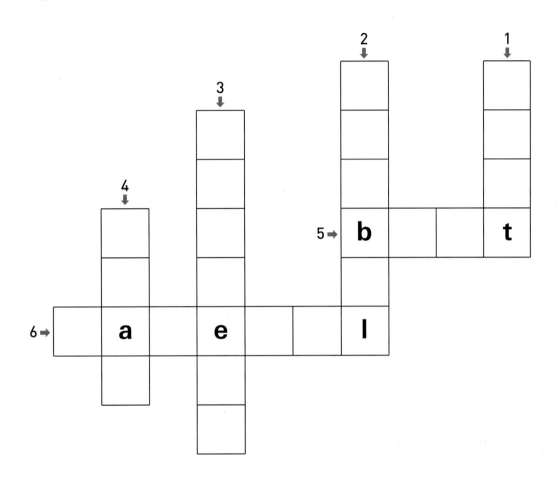

#	Korean	
1	다친	_____
2	상징	_____
3	주말	_____
4	시험	_____
5	가장 좋은	_____
6	조심하는	_____

C Fill in the blank.

1 네 생일은 언제니?

_____ is your birthday?

2 너는 언제 학교에 가니?

_____ do you go to school?

3 너는 언제 일을 끝낼 거니?

_____ will you finish your work?

D Unscramble the words to make a sentence.

1 너는 언제 올 수 있니?

you	when	come	can

_____ ?

2 너는 언제 일어나니?

up	do	when	you	get

_____ ?

3 너는 언제 썰매 타러 갈 거니?

go	will	you	when	sledding

_____ ?

E Fill in the blank.

1 내 생일은 설날이야.

My birthday is _____ New Year's Day.

2 나는 일요일에 부모님을 뵈러 갈 거야.

I'll visit my parents _____ Sunday.

3 우리는 8시에 아침 식사를 해.

We have breakfast _____ 8 o'clock.

F Unscramble the words to make a sentence.

1 나는 주말마다 농구를 해.

| basketball | I | weekends | on | play |

_____ .

2 그녀는 7시에 파티를 열 거야.

| 7 o'clock | have | she'll | a party | at |

_____ .

3 그 새는 밤에 잠을 자지 않아.

| night | the bird | sleep | doesn't | at |

_____ .

G Listen and write the word. 🎧 T30

1 _____

2 _____

3 _____

4 _____

5 _____

6 _____

7 _____

H Listen and fill in the blanks. 🎧 T31

1 _____ will you do your _____?

2 My birthday is _____.

3 I usually go to school _____.

4 I like to read the _____.

5 _____ cars and water.

6 Do not _____.